Nature School

LET'S LOOK FOR FLOWERS!

By Seth Lynch

Gareth Stevens
PUBLISHING

Please visit our website, www.garethstevens.com. For a free color catalog of all our high-quality books, call toll free 1-800-542-2595 or fax 1-877-542-2596.

Library of Congress Cataloging-in-Publication Data

Names: Lynch, Seth, author.
Title: Let's look for flowers! / Seth Lynch.
Description: Buffalo, New York : Gareth Stevens Publishing, [2024] |
    Series: Nature school | Includes index. | Audience: Grades K-1
Identifiers: LCCN 2022045096 (print) | LCCN 2022045097 (ebook) | ISBN
    9781538286234 (library binding) | ISBN 9781538286227 (paperback) | ISBN
    9781538286241 (ebook)
Subjects: LCSH: Flowers–Juvenile literature.
Classification: LCC QK653 .L96 2024 (print) | LCC QK653 (ebook) | DDC
    575.6–dc23/eng/20221012
LC record available at https://lccn.loc.gov/2022045096
LC ebook record available at https://lccn.loc.gov/2022045097

First Edition

Published in 2024 by
Gareth Stevens Publishing
2544 Clinton St,
Buffalo, NY 14224

Editor: Kristen Nelson
Designer: Andrea Davison-Bartolotta; Claire Wrazin

Photo credits: Cover Lulub/Shutterstock.com; p. 1 Dajra/Shutterstock.com; p. 5 Tohuwabohu1976/ Shutterstock.com; pp. 7, 24 (petal) Vasilyev Alexandr/Shutterstock.com; p. 9 Gardarikanec/Shutterstock.com; pp. 11, 24 (stem) Karuna Tansuk/Shutterstock.com; p. 13 Flower_Garden/Shutterstock.com; p. 15 Filipe B. Varela/Shutterstock.com; p. 17 TeleMakro Fotografie/Shutterstock.com; p. 19 Brian A Jackson/ Shutterstock.com; p. 21 Gavrusha/Shutterstock.com; p. 23 Eugene Kovalchuk/Shutterstock.com; p. 24 (prickle) Anton-Burakov/Shutterstock.com.

Printed in the United States of America

CPSIA compliance information: Batch #CS24GS: For further information contact Gareth Stevens, New York, New York at 1-800-542-2595.

Find us on

Contents

Let's look for flowers.
They grow on plants.

They have petals.
These can be
many colors.

We see a daisy.
It is yellow.

Flowers have leaves and stems.

A rose has small leaves.
It has sharp prickles.

13

Flowers have roots.
These take in water.

Seeds form
inside flowers.
They grow into
new plants.

We see a dandelion.
Wind blows seeds away.

19

Apple trees grow flowers. They are white and pink.

21

They become fruit.

Words to Know

petal

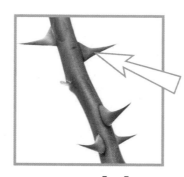
prickle

stem

Index